Bradley Tice

Cryptography and Quantum Computing: Securing Business Information

GRIN Verlag

Bibliografische Information der Deutschen Nationalbibliothek:

Die Deutsche Bibliothek verzeichnet diese Publikation in der Deutschen National-
bibliografie; detaillierte bibliografische Daten sind im Internet über http://dnb.d-
nb.de/ abrufbar.

Imprint:

Copyright © 2004 GRIN Verlag GmbH
Druck und Bindung: Books on Demand GmbH, Norderstedt Germany
ISBN: 978-3-656-35194-8

GRIN - Your knowledge has value

Der GRIN Verlag publiziert seit 1998 wissenschaftliche Arbeiten von Studenten, Hochschullehrern und anderen Akademikern als eBook und gedrucktes Buch. Die Verlagswebsite www.grin.com ist die ideale Plattform zur Veröffentlichung von Hausarbeiten, Abschlussarbeiten, wissenschaftlichen Aufsätzen, Dissertationen und Fachbüchern.

Visit us on the internet:

http://www.grin.com/

http://www.facebook.com/grincom

http://www.twitter.com/grin_com

Cryptography and Quantum Computing: Securing Business
Information

A Dissertation Submitted for the Doctor of
Philosophy in Theocentric Business and Ethics
Degree from the American College of Metaphysical
Theology

March 6, 2004

Dr. Bradley S. Tice

Abstract

The dissertation will address the use of cryptography in quantum computing to develop a secure system for storage and transmission of business information.

Preface

The dissertation will examine the nature of quantum computing and quantum cryptography for the private sector as it relates to the use of 'secure storage and transmission' of business information. While quantum computing is very much in its early stages and is not, as yet, a mainstream operational system, the basic units and codes around those basic units of quantum information are, at a theoretical level at least, of a practical nature.

Second Preface

The revision of the original dissertation has allowed for a more clear analysis of the basics of quantum computing and better models to describe basic quantum units for secure coding.

Sincerely,

Dr. Bradley S. Tice, FRSS

July 10, 2012

The Table of Contents

Introduction

The dissertation will examine the use of cryptography and quantum computing to secure business information for storage and transmission. The start of modern machine coding for business came after World War One by the way of a German electrical engineer named Arthur Scherbius (Kahn, 1991: 31). Scherbius took advantage of Germany's vast Post-War publication of both private and public commercial codes for business (Kahn, 1991: 35).

Originally designed to save on 'telegraph calls' these secret codes did have a measure of privacy in transmission (Kahn, 1991: 35). What made Scherbius' electrical 'encipher' machine special was the 'rotating' code wheels that could be interchanged to add to the length of the coded message (Kahn, 1991: 32-33). These commercial coding machines became the proto-types for the Naval and Army 'Enigma' coding machines of World War Two (Kahn, 1991: 43).

The need for secret, or private, correspondence in the field of business is never more important to day as it was in the early 20th century. With the coming advent of practical quantum computers, the use of 'quantum information' is a viable vehicle for coded messages of the future.

This dissertation will examine quantum computing and the growing field of cryptography in quantum computing. The focus of the monograph is in the use of cryptography in quantum computing for secure business information storage and transmission. This will be done by the examination of various Pauli gate matrix's and the three state qutrit. The methodology to be used in the repetition of specific qubit and qutrit matrix's and provide a secure transmission cell of extensive duplication and redundancy within the coded message.

The Review of Literature

The literature used for this dissertation is concise. The
Wikipedia encyclopedia entries are foundational for the examples
that are used in forming the quantum cryptography codes and is
based on legitimate scholarly references as found on the site
(Wikipedia, 2012a and 2012b).

Kahn (1991) is an excellent source for the history of World War
Two coding information as well as a general history of secret
codes as found in his The Codebreakers: The Story of Secret
Writing (New York: MacMillan, 1967). Shannon and Weaver's
monograph (1949) details Shannon's interest in cryptography and
statistical communication theory (Shannon and Weaver, 1949).

The author's unpublished manuscript An Abstract on the Theory
and Application for a Universal Archetype Computer contains the
first work by the author on quantum computers and cryptography
and is the source of the examples given in this dissertation
(Tice, 2012).

Pfeifer (2007) is used for the description of quantum computing
and Schneier (1996) and Meyer and Matyas (1982) examine rates of
entropy in meaningful messages. Patterson (1987) describes the
'Playfair' square cipher and Singh (1999) examines the
historical context to that cipher.

Quantum Computing

Quantum computing uses atomic particles that function as time
sensitive locations, per atom, for computations (Pfeifer, 2007:
676). The field of quantum computing was founded by Richard
Feynman in 1982 (Wikipedia, 2012c: 1). The use of qubits,
instead of classical computing's bits, in quantum computers
represents (n) qubits in an arbitrary superposition of up to
2(n) different states simultaneously and operates by setting the
qubits into an initial state that is controlled and maintained
by a fixed sequence of quantum logic gates (Wikipedia, 2012c,
2). The qubits follow only a 'probabilistic' superposition of
states that is measured at one point only and not the actual
superposition states before and after the measurement
(Wikipedia, 2012c, 2).

The focus of this dissertation is on quantum logic gates and
cryptography. The premise of this monograph is the historically
valid use of repetition and redundancy found in linear codes of
the alpha-numeric variety.

Shannon has noted that the English language is highly redundant
and that many words have very high levels of frequency, or rate
of repetition (Shannon and Weaver, 1949:39-44). Patterson
(1987) notes that the classic Playfair square cipher is not

'vulnerable' to frequency analysis because there is no one to one ratio to each letter of a word, the use of multiple letters to signify a single letter in the code, were as, phrase to phrase ratios are open to frequency analysis (Patterson, 1987: 13 and Note #1). Patterson (1987) discusses the Playfair cipher and Singh (1999) gives a the history of this interesting cipher. Meyer and Matyas (1982) defines the averages of a 'meaningful text' in common passages of English and Schneier (1996) explains the rate of language and entropy.

Cryptography and the Quantum Gate

The quantum gate is a reversible 'logic' gate that uses a 'qubit' as its basic unit of measure (Wikipedia 2012a, 1-2). Like the nomenclature of a binary system that uses the 'bit' as representing the basic unit of that system the 'qubit' is a reversible system of simultaneous states (Wikipedia, 2012a, 1-2). The Pauli X gate is a common gate found in quantum computing and employs a single qubit in the Pauli X matrix that has as its 4 character form a 0 to 1 and a 1 to 0 matrix (Wikipedia, 2012a, 2).

Pauli X Matrix

$$X = \begin{matrix} 0 & 1 \\ 1 & 0 \end{matrix}$$

The use of repetition in cryptography is quite old and is used to 'deceive' the interceptor of the code by allowing for 'too much information' in the coded message and hence, provide an 'extraneous' amount of information to decode. The number of characters used in the code can be increased along with the chromatic aspects of the message, from simple black and white to color, and that can impart more states that the original information had to add to the 'amount' of information to be 'decoded'.

A Modified Pauli X Matrix could be as follows:

Modified Pauli X Matrix

$$X = \begin{matrix} 01110010 \\ 10001101 \end{matrix}$$

The true value of this coded dual sequence is the last two upper and lower matrix numbers as follows:

$$X = \begin{matrix} 10 \\ 01 \end{matrix}$$

The Pauli Y gate functions on a singular qubit and represents a 0 to i/1 and /1 to -i/0 matrix(Wikipedia, 2012a: 2). A Pauli Y gate matrix is as follows:

12

Pauli Y Gate Matrix

$$Y = \begin{matrix} 0 & -i \\ i & 0 \end{matrix}$$

A Modified Pauli Y gate matrix would be the following series of upper and lower matrix codes:

Modified Pauli Y Gate Matrix

$$\begin{matrix} 0 & i & 0 & 0 & -i & 0 & i & 0 & 0 \\ i & 0 & 0 & i & 0 & 0 & -i & 0 \end{matrix}$$

With the 4th and 5th characters of both the upper and lower lines being the correct qubit sequence.
Not to be left out of the Pauli gates is the Pauli Z gate that functions on a single qubit and represents a an unchanged basis state 0 and defines 1 to -/1 matrix (Wikipedia, 2012a: 2). A

Pauli Z gate matrix is as follows:

Pauli Z Gate Matrix

Z = 1 0
    0 -1

The Modified Pauli Z Gate Matrix is as follows:

Modified Pauli Z Gate Matrix

0 0 0 0 0 1 -1 1 0 0 1
0 1-1-1 1 0 1 0-1 1 0

The 8th and 9th characters on both lines are the correct qubit.

Cryptography and The Qutrit

The 'Qutrit' is a three state or ternary system and represents three, 3, different states simultaneously (Wikipedia, 2012b, 1-2). The use of a three character system can use the Arabic numerals [0, 1 and 2] to represent the three states as follows (Tice, 2012: 38):

Basic Qutrit Unit

012

Like the use of 'extaneous' repetitions of a basic qubit, the same type of duplication in a linear manner would be as follows:

Coded Basic Qutrit Unit

012012012012012012012012012

The first three qutrit numbers are the original message. The use of chromatic, or color, beyond the basic black and white, monotone or monochromatic, aspect to the code would enhance the 'amount' of information in the code and add to the total amount of information imparted in the coded message (Tice, 2012: 40).

Conclusion

The use of repetition in linear qubit gate matrix's and qutrits allows for an extension of both duplication, redundancy's, and specialized corruption of the message by similar, but different information in the coded message. The use of these theoretical models for future use in securing business information is proposed in this monograph.

Summary

The dissertation has presented research in the area of business communications for securing such information in a secure message. While the monograph is theoretical in nature, and at present there are no operation quantum computers beyond the laboratory stage, the work in this dissertation has potential for the design of quantum information cryptography systems for the future.

Notes

[1]. Simon Singh (1999) gives an interesting account of the development of the 'Playfair' cipher that started as coded messages in the personal columns of English newspapers during Victorian times. These 'private codes' became the interest of amateur cryptanalysis

(Singh, 1999: 79-80).

References

Kahn, D. (1991) Seizing the Enigma.
New York: Barnes and Noble Books.

Meyer, C.H. and Matyas, S.M. (1982) Cryptography: A New Dimension in Computer Data Security. New York: John Wiley & Sons.

Patterson, W. (1987) Mathematical Cryptology for Computer Scientists and Mathematicains. :Rowman and Littlefield

Pfeifer, P. (2007) McGraw-Hill Encyclopedia of Science & Technology.
Volume 14 PLAS-QUI, New York: McGraw-Hill.

Schneier, B. (1996) Applied Cryptography.
New York: John Wiley & Sons, Inc.

Shannon, C.E. and Weaver, W. (1949) The Mathematical Theory of Communication. Champaign Illinois: University of Illinois.

Singh, S. (1999) The Code Book.
New York: Doubleday.

Tice, B.S. (2012) An Abstract on the Theory and Application of a Universal Archetype Computer. Unpublished Manuscript. Copyright 2012.

Wikipedia (2012a) "Quantum Gate".
Website: http://en.wikipedia.org/wiki/Quantum_gate

Wikipedia (2012b) "Qutrit".
Website: http://en.wikipedia.org/wiki/Qutrit

Wikipedia (2012c) "Quantum computer".
Website: http://en.wikipedia.org/wiki/Quantum computers

About The Author

Dr. Tice is the CEO of Advanced Human Design, a research and development company located in The Central Valley of Northern California, U.S.A. Dr. Tice is, or has been, a member of the following Societies: ACM, IEEE, SIAM, AMS and is a Fellow of The Royal Statistical Society and a Fellow of The British Computer Society.